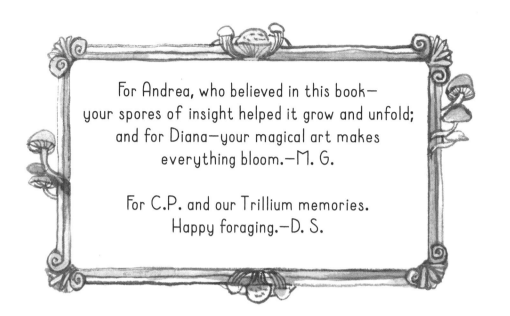

For Andrea, who believed in this book—
your spores of insight helped it grow and unfold;
and for Diana—your magical art makes
everything bloom.—M. G.

For C.P. and our Trillium memories.
Happy foraging.—D. S.

BEACH LANE BOOKS
An imprint of Simon & Schuster Children's Publishing Division
1230 Avenue of the Americas, New York, New York 10020
Text © 2023 by Maria Gianferrari
Illustration © 2023 by Diana Sudyka
Book design by Lauren Rille © 2023 by Simon & Schuster, Inc.
BEACH LANE BOOKS and colophon are trademarks of Simon & Schuster, Inc.
For information about special discounts for bulk purchases, please contact Simon & Schuster Special Sales
at 1-866-506-1949 or business@simonandschuster.com.
The Simon & Schuster Speakers Bureau can bring authors to your live event. For more information or to book an event,
contact the Simon & Schuster Speakers Bureau at 1-866-248-3049 or visit our website at www.simonspeakers.com.
The text for this book was set in Catalina.
The illustrations for this book were rendered in gouache watercolor and finished digitally.
Manufactured in China
1223 SCP
10 9 8 7 6 5 4 3 2
Library of Congress Cataloging-in-Publication Data • Names: Gianferrari, Maria, author. | Sudyka, Diana, illustrator. • Title: Fungi grow / Maria
Gianferrari ; Illustrated by Diana Sudyka. •Description: First edition. | New York, NY : Beach Lane Books, an imprint of Simon & Schuster Children's
Publishing Division, [2023] | Includes bibliographical references. | Audience: Ages 4-8 | Audience: Grades 2-3 | Summary: "Fungi are all around us.
Some are edible, and some are poisonous. Some help forests communicate, others recycle decaying matter. But all across the world, fungi are
growing. Discover when, how, where, and why in this poetic and illuminating nonfiction picture book"— Provided by publisher. • Identifiers: LCCN
2022046623 | ISBN 9781665903653 (hardcover) | ISBN 9781665903660 (ebook) • Subjects: LCSH: Fungi—Juvenile literature. • Classification:
LCC QK603.5 .G53 2023 | DDC 579.5—dc23/eng/20221003 • LC record available at https://lccn.loc.gov/2022046623

Special thanks to mycologist Morgan Rockwell for his expert review of this book.

FUNGI GROW

by Maria Gianferrari

Illustrated by Diana Sudyka

Beach Lane Books

New York London Toronto Sydney New Delhi

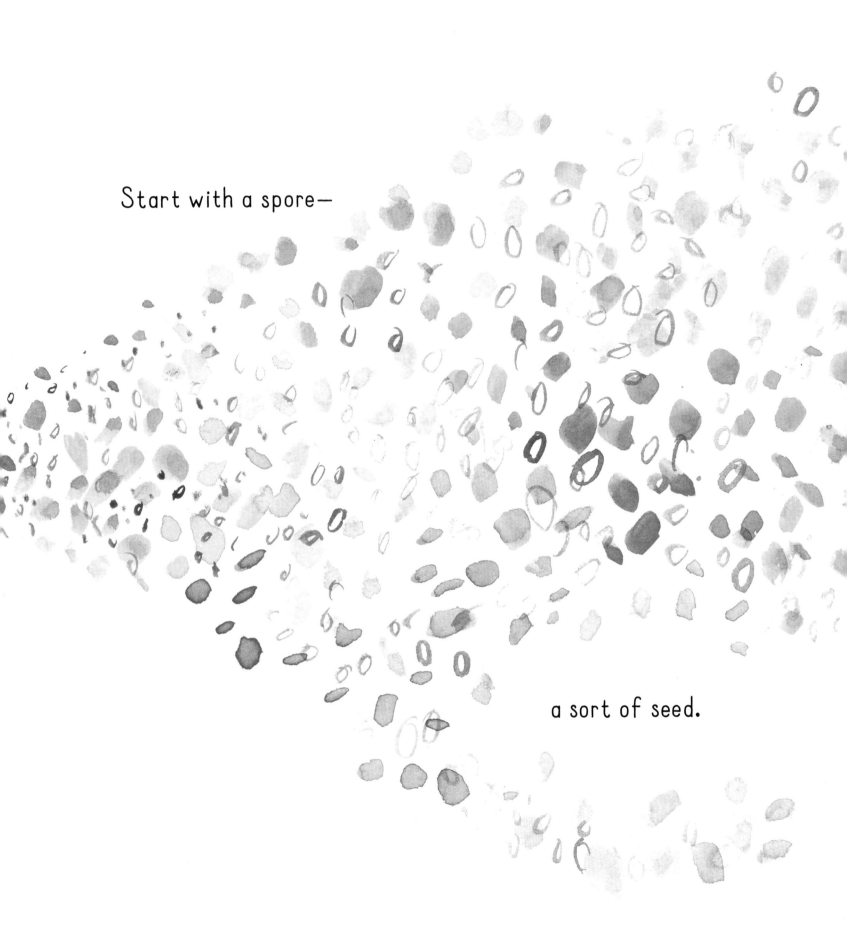

Start with a spore—

a sort of seed.

Spores shoot

Indigo milk cap

from gills

Hedgehog mushroom

or teeth

Bolete

or pores.

Spores catapult, sail, wander with wind.

PUFF!

Violet cort

Cottony rot fungus spurts plumes of spores. This action, called "puffing," creates wind for spores to sail on.

Cottony rot fungus

PLOP!

Some spores spread
when raindrops drop.

Rooted collybia

Bird's nest fungi spores are dispersed
by falling raindrops.

Bird's nest fungus

POOF!

Others spurt out like clouds of smoke.

Pear-shaped puffball

When people or animals step on puffball mushrooms, spores surge out like smoke from tiny openings called ostioles. Pelting rain can also discharge puffball spores.

PEE-EW!

Some spores spread
with stink and slime.

Dog stinkhorn

Stinkhorn mushrooms produce
a slime smelling of rotten meat
to attract flies. The flies feed,
get coated in slime, and spread
spores when they fly away.

Some travel on
creatures
(or through them).

Then . . .

Yellow morel

When animals consume mushrooms, some spores
spread through their poop. Other spores travel
on feet, feathers, or fur.

Fungi grow.

Finding moisture,
spores take root.

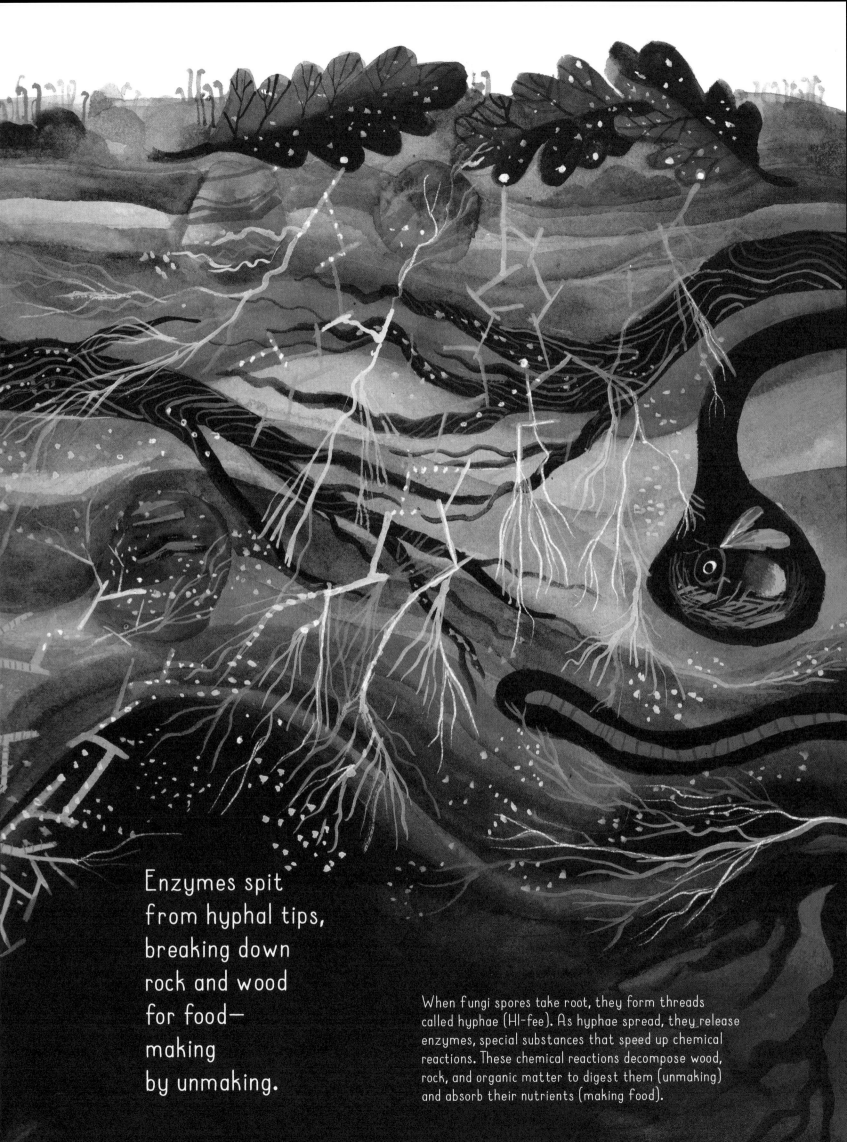

Enzymes spit
from hyphal tips,
breaking down
rock and wood
for food—
making
by unmaking.

When fungi spores take root, they form threads
called hyphae (HI-fee). As hyphae spread, they release
enzymes, special substances that speed up chemical
reactions. These chemical reactions decompose wood,
rock, and organic matter to digest them (unmaking)
and absorb their nutrients (making food).

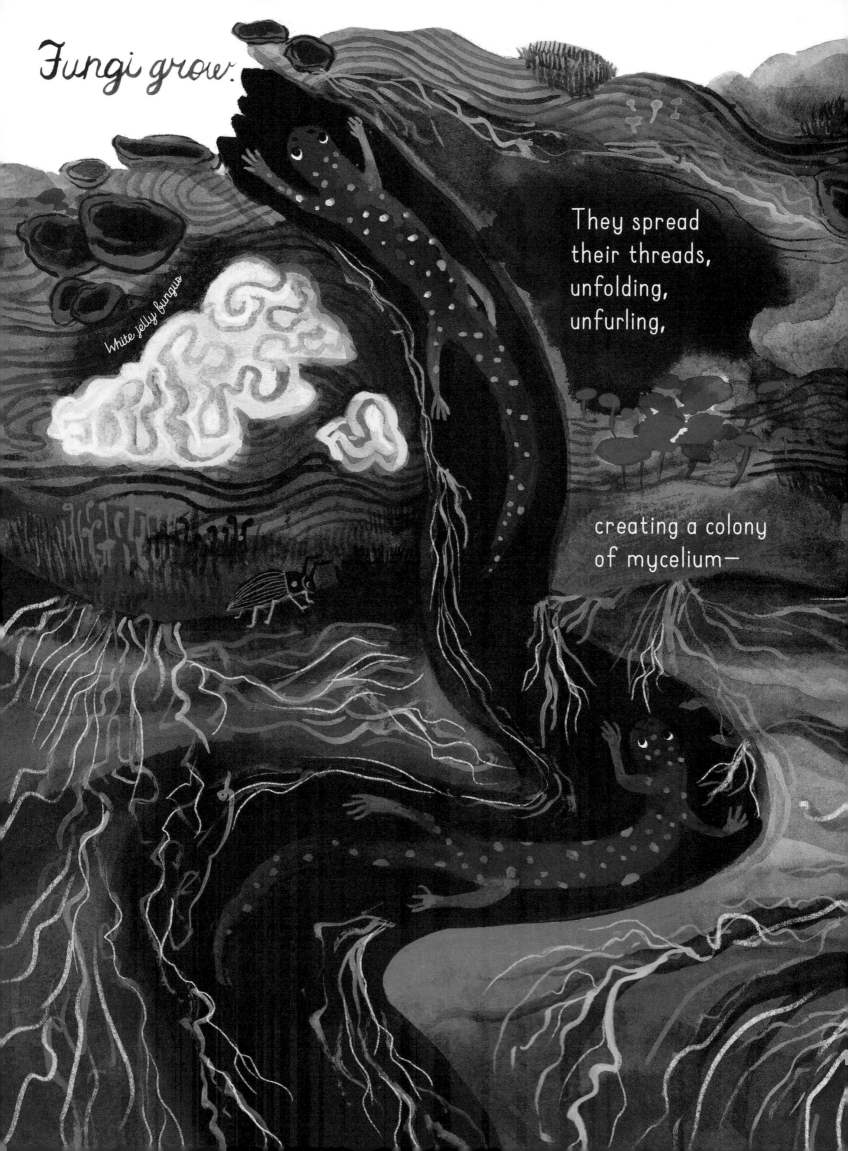

Fungi grow.

White jelly fungus

They spread
their threads,
unfolding,
unfurling,

creating a colony
of mycelium—

Wood ears

Crown-tipped coral

a knitted network
of roots.

Hyphae form the mycelium (my-SEE-lee-um), the part of the fungus
that lives underground. The mycelium is made up of cottony threads that
can produce mushrooms aboveground. The area beneath a single footprint
in the forest can contain hundreds of miles of mycelium! Compared with
plants, mushrooms are the flowers, the fruiting bodies of a fungus,
whereas mycelium is like roots.

Fungi grow.

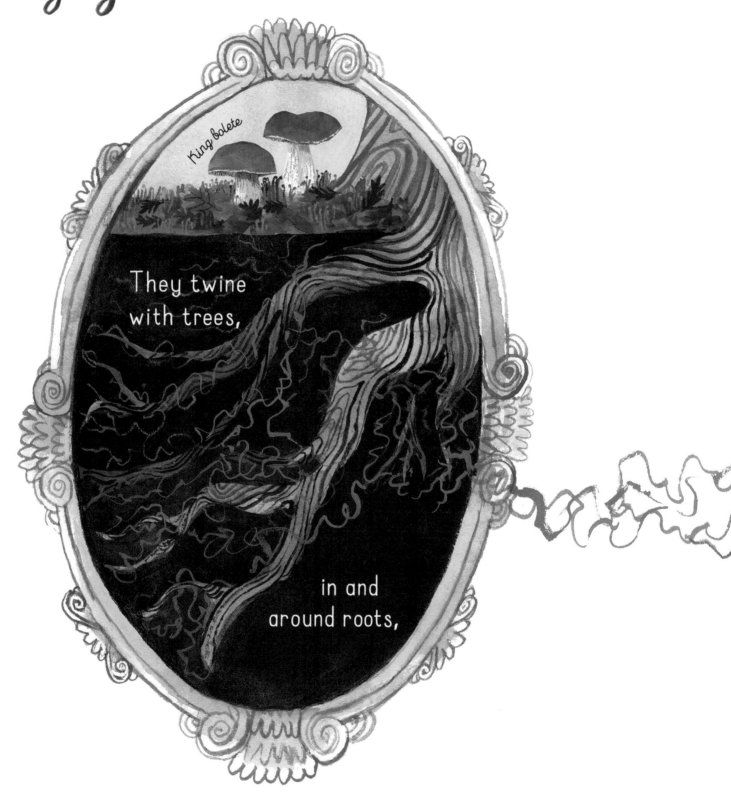

King bolete

They twine
with trees,

in and
around roots,

Pine mushroom

mining for
minerals.

Mycorrhizal (my-kuh-RYE-zal) fungi is a type of
fungi that winds in and around tree roots and forms a
mutually beneficial relationship with trees. They cannot
create the sugar they need to grow, so they partner
with trees. The fungi mine minerals from the soil to
share with trees; the trees collect water, sunlight,
and carbon dioxide to make sugar, which they share
with the fungi.

Fungi grow.

They fuse
forest trees together
through their roots,
so trees can talk,
share,
store,
and warn,
keeping the forest
healthy
and in balance.

Mycelium: root . . .

Trees in a forest are connected through a "wood-wide web," an underground network of mycorrhizal fungi that helps them to communicate using chemical, hormonal, and electrical signals. The trees share and store water and resources and warn of dangers, like insect infestations, all through the fungal network. Mother trees are often the center of this hub and can be connected to hundreds of other trees, including their seedlings growing in the forest understory.

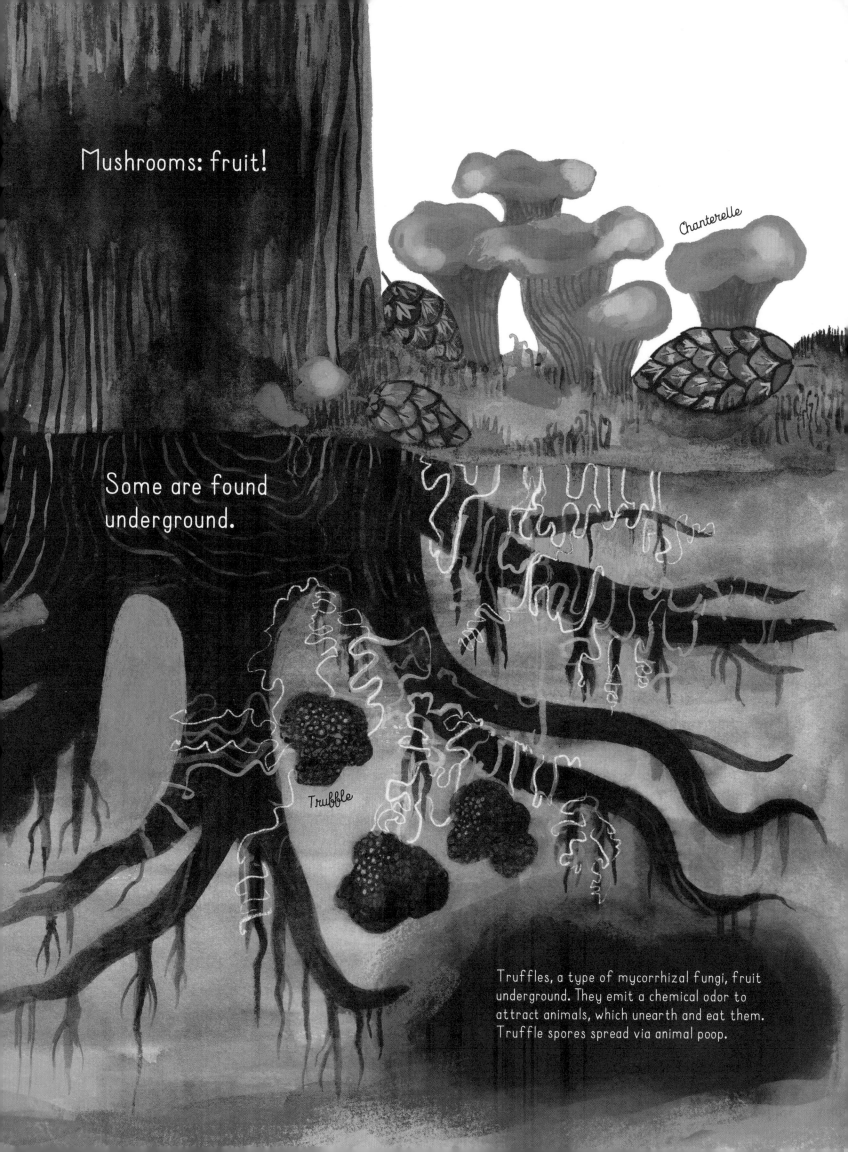

Mushrooms: fruit!

Chanterelle

Some are found underground.

Truffle

Truffles, a type of mycorrhizal fungi, fruit underground. They emit a chemical odor to attract animals, which unearth and eat them. Truffle spores spread via animal poop.

Some stalks surface,

swell,

stretch.

Then veils lift.

Deer mushroom

Saprotrophic mushrooms are decomposers, growing on decaying wood, plants, and animals.

And from dead stuff,

mushrooms erupt!

Artist's bracket

Mushrooms SPROUT.

Pinwheel mushroom

Parasols POP OUT.

Orange pinwheel

Red pinwheel

Rusty-gilled polypore

Violet-toothed polypore

Turkey tail

Mushrooms fan,
arc,
spread their skirts.

SPLASH,

and

SWIRL.

Scarlet cups

Yellow fairy cups

Witch's butter

Amber jelly roll fungus

Mushrooms

BEWITCH,

Lion's mane

Chicken of the woods

Red cage fungus

Devil's urn

Fungi grow.

They flourish
and thrive . . .

Shaggy ink cap

The shaggy ink cap mushroom is tough enough to
crack asphalt and cement. Sprouting mushrooms
rapidly absorb water, and this force of pressure
helps them displace weight like a hydraulic jack:
pop go the mushrooms!

where plants can't.

A black fungus nicknamed "Hulk bugs" flourishes at Chernobyl, the site of a nuclear reactor accident, and seems to use harmful gamma ray radiation as an energy source, like plants use sunlight for growth.

Fungi grow.

Destroying angel

Skullcap dapperling

They poison
and kill . . .

Death cap

Fly amanita

Deadly webcap

Many poisonous mushrooms will make you sick, but death caps can actually kill you! After eating them, victims experience food-poisoning-like symptoms such as nausea and diarrhea. Severe dehydration can lead to liver failure. In that case, the only chance at survival is a liver transplant.

Cordyceps

Zombie ant fungus is found in tropical rain forests. It infects ants by invading their bodies and brains. The fungus controls the ant's brain, forcing it to leave its nest and lock its jaw onto a leaf. After the ant dies, a mushroom pops out of its head, and spores spread to the ant colony below, where the fungus infects even more ants.

and prey upon.

Honey fungus

Honey fungus spreads under a tree's bark and rots its roots, preventing the flow of nutrients. Trees starve and dehydrate. The Blue Mountains in eastern Oregon are home to a honey fungus colony that spans nearly four square miles. It is believed to be the world's largest single organism—the size of three blue whales—and is thousands of years old.

Parasitic fungi use living organisms for food.

But fungi also heal . . .

Penicillium mold

PENICILLIN ANTIBIOTIC

Mold, a type of fungus, can be developed into antibiotics to kill bacteria that cause disease. One of the earliest developed antibiotics, penicillin, comes from the mold penicillium.

ANTIVIRAL

Agarikon

Agarikon, a fungus found in the old-growth forests of the Pacific Northwest, grows in conifer trees and can live up to seventy-five years. Strains of this mushroom have been effective in fighting flu and pox viruses.

and help!

Oyster mushroom

Fungi are master recyclers. They use enzymes and acids to break down dead and decaying matter for food. This process creates new soil and enriches existing soil.

Some enzymes are so powerful that they can digest pollutants like petroleum, biological and chemical waste, and even heavy metals.

Fungi grow.

Sometimes slow.

When environmental conditions aren't quite right (not enough food or moisture), some spores can enter dormancy, a sleeplike state, and stay that way until conditions improve for growth.

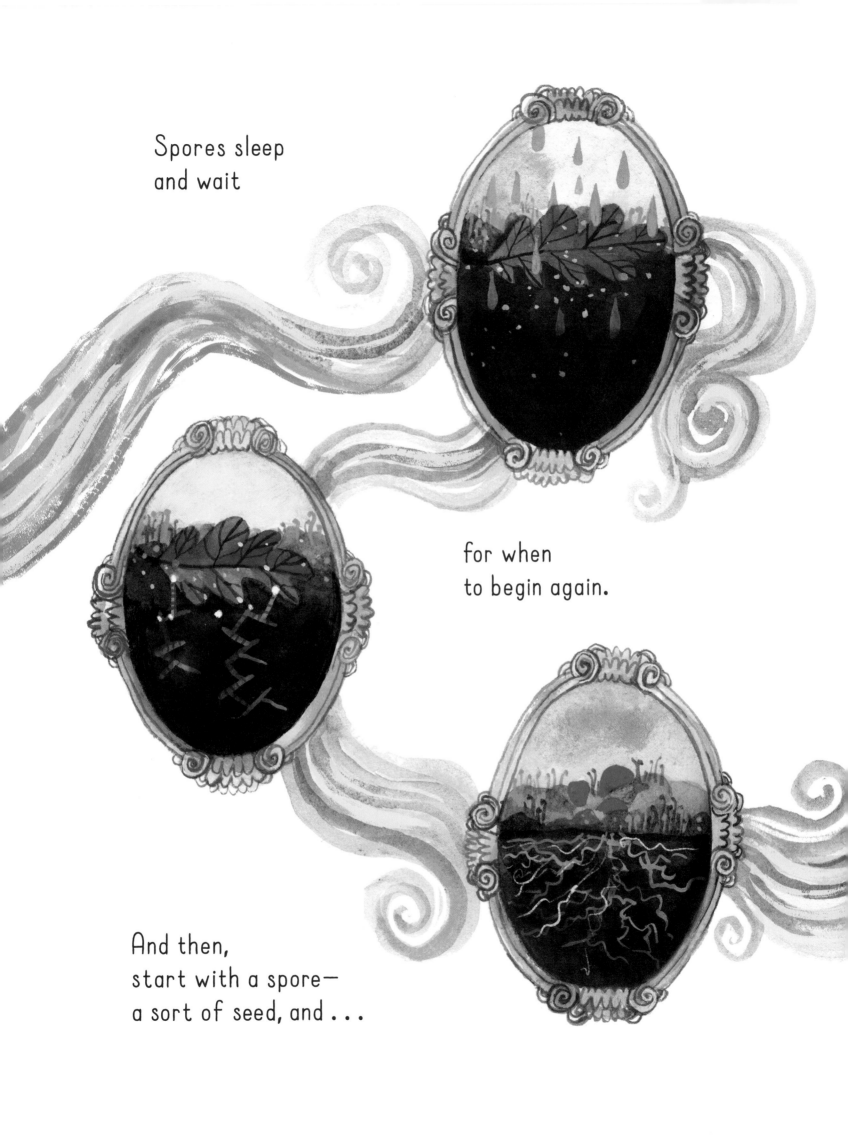

Spores sleep
and wait

for when
to begin again.

And then,
start with a spore—
a sort of seed, and . . .

Fungi grow!

WARNING!

NEVER eat mushrooms that you've found outside unless their identity is verified by a mycologist, an expert in mushrooms. The mushrooms could be poisonous. Many poisonous mushrooms look very similar to edible ones.

GLOSSARY

fungi (FUN-guy or FUN-jie): spore-producing organisms that are classified as their own kingdom, separate from plants and animals

hyphae (HI-fee): threads of a fungal body that, in their search for nutrients, branch into a network of mycelium

mushrooms: the fruiting bodies of fungi

mycelium (my-SEE-lee-um): the nutrient-gathering part of a fungus consisting of hyphae

mycology (my-KAH-luh-jee): a branch of biology dealing with fungi

mycorrhiza (my-cuh-RYE-zah): this word means "fungal root" and is a kind of mutually beneficial relationship between a fungus and a plant

spores: particles produced by mushrooms to disperse and reproduce new mushrooms

HOW FUNGI HEAL AND HELP

Fungi are sustainable: they recycle, clean, and protect the environment.

Mycoremediation: This is the process of using fungi to break down agricultural, industrial, and chemical waste.

- Digesting petroleum/oil: Straw mats inoculated (filled) with mycelium spores can absorb oils, break down their hydrocarbon bonds, and convert the hydrocarbons into energy. Out sprout oyster mushrooms!

- Breaking down plastics: One of the main ingredients in plastic is crude-oil-processed petroleum. It may take hundreds of years for plastic to degrade. Scientists working in China discovered a fungus, *Aspergillus tubingensis*, at a waste site in Pakistan that in only two months broke down polyurethane, a plastic used in refrigerator insulation and fake leather. Students at Yale University discovered *Pestalotiopsis microspora* in the Amazon that also eats polyurethane.

- Filtering farm/chemical waste: Sacks inoculated with mycelium spores act like filters and can be placed downstream from farms and factories to absorb bacterial waste like *E. coli*, chemical fertilizer waste, and even toxic heavy metal contamination, a process known as *mycofiltration*.

Insect management

Instead of using insecticides made from harmful chemicals, use mushrooms or mycopesticides! The classic fly agaric or fly amanita mushroom placed in a saucer of milk can attract and kill flies.

Mycologist Paul Stamets has also developed fungus-based insecticides to kill carpenter ants using mycelium before it produces spores. Ants eat the fungus and their bodies become mummified. Mushrooms pop out of their heads!

Preserving pollinators

Honeybees are important pollinators of food crops. The honeybee population is under threat from the *Varroa* mite, a parasite. The mites lay eggs in beehive cells and feed on their larvae and pupae as well as adult and baby honeybees, which damages their bodies and affects their abilities to forage. They also spread viruses such as deformed wing virus. Paul Stamets and Steve Sheppard, a scientist at Washington State University, worked together to develop a mycelium extract that reduced viruses in bees. It also prolonged their lives, perhaps due to increased immunity.

Partnering with trees

Mycorrhizal fungi form a partnership—a symbiotic (sim-bee-AH-tick) relationship—with trees and other plants that is mutually beneficial, known as the "wood-wide web." Fungi colonize the tree's roots and share with the trees any minerals and nutrients they mine from the soil. In exchange, the trees share with the fungi the sugar (carbon) that they collect through photosynthesis, which is essential because fungi cannot make their own sugar.

Fungi mine for minerals by worming their threads through the spaces between soil particles too small for tree roots, searching for rocks. They secrete acid to dissolve the rocks' surfaces, then tunnel inside and mine out minerals such as nitrogen, phosphorus, magnesium, potassium, and calcium, which they send to the tree's roots.

Fungi share resources with trees in other ways too. They prey upon flea-like insects called springtails, which are decomposers that live in soil and leaf litter. Fungi burrow into the springtails' nitrogen-rich bodies, and then they share the nitrogen with trees. In the Pacific Northwest region of North America, fungi seek decomposing salmon remains in the soil as a nitrogen source. Much of the nitrogen found in this area's trees comes from fish.

FUN FUNGI FACTS

- Mushrooms can sprout and double in size in just twenty-four hours! Plants and animals grow when cells in their bodies divide, and that takes time. Many mushrooms, especially gilled mushrooms, grow from cell enlargement. Their cells balloon by absorbing water, which takes less energy than cell division.

- Mushrooms grown indoors and on farms are called "cultivated" mushrooms. Most of our nation's cultivated mushrooms are grown on farms in Pennsylvania.

- The white button mushroom is the most common mushroom eaten in the US. Nearly all of today's white button mushrooms originated from a spore strain created by Dutch scientist Gerda Fritsche in 1980.

- According to the American Mushroom Institute, it only takes about two gallons of water to grow a pound of mushrooms. It takes over fifty gallons of water to grow other kinds of produce. And they don't need much space to grow—one acre of land can produce millions of mushrooms.

- Mycelium can be molded into eco-friendly packaging material that can be composted. Say goodbye to Bubble Wrap and Styrofoam peanuts. You can even plant it in your garden!

- A very small percentage of the world's fungi have been identified—there are millions more species waiting to be discovered. Maybe *you'll* discover some!

FUNGI LIFE CYCLE*

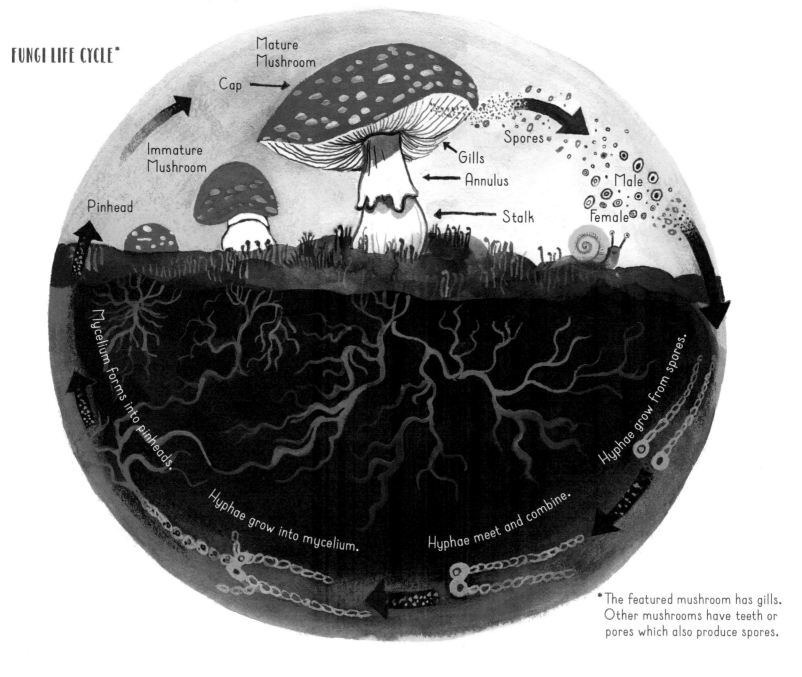

*The featured mushroom has gills. Other mushrooms have teeth or pores which also produce spores.

SOURCES

Bone, Eugenia. *Mycophilia: Revelations from the Weird World of Mushrooms*. New York: Rodale, Inc., 2011.

Phillips, Roger. *Mushrooms and Other Fungi of North America*. Buffalo: Firefly Books, Ltd., 2005.

Sheldrake, Merlin. *Entangled Life: How Fungi Make Our Worlds, Change Our Minds & Shape Our Futures*. New York: Random House, 2020.

Stamets, Paul, ed. *Fantastic Fungi: How Mushrooms Can Heal, Shift Consciousness, and Save the Planet*. San Rafael, California: Earth Aware Editions, 2019.

Stamets, Paul. *Mycelium Running: How Mushrooms Can Help Save the World*. Berkeley: Ten Speed Press, 2005.

FURTHER READING FOR KIDS

Boddy, Lynne. *Humongous Fungus*. New York: DK, 2021.

Gabriel, Alisha, and Sue Heavenrich. *Funky Fungi*. Chicago: Chicago Review Press, 2022.

Keller, Joy. *Fungus is Among Us!* Seattle: The Innovation Press, 2019.

Gaya, Ester. *Fungarium*. Somerville: Big Picture Press, 2021.

Gravel, Elise. *The Mushroom Fan Club*. Montreal: Enfant, 2018.

Zimmerman, Laura. *Mushroom Rain*. Ann Arbor: Sleeping Bear Press, 2022.

ADDITIONAL RESOURCES

Bradt, Steve, and Bob Sanders. "More from Spores: How They Spread." Harvard Gazette, September 27, 2010. https://news.harvard.edu/gazette/story/2010/09 /more-from-spores-how-they-spread.

Denhof, Sarah. "The Mycorrhizal Network: How Trees Secretly Talk to Each Other." YUP, February 18, 2019. https:// yupthatexists.com/the-mycorrhizal-network.

Garcia-Pardo, Gabriella, producer. "You Didn't Know Mushrooms Could Do All This." *National Geographic*, July 13, 2016. https://www.youtube.com/watch?v=BlcKBKJ8uro.

Schwartzberg, Louie, director. *Fantastic Fungi*. https:// fantasticfungi.com/film.

Simard, Suzanne. "How Trees Talk to Each Other." Filmed June 2016 in Banff, Alberta, Canada. TED video, 18:10. https://www.ted.com/talks/suzanne_simard_how _trees_talk_to_each_other.

Stamets, Paul. "6 Ways Mushrooms Can Save the World." Filmed February 2008 in Monterey, California. TED video, 17:25. https://www.ted.com/talks/paul_stamets _on_6_ways_mushrooms_can_save_the_world.

"The Wood Wide Web: How Trees Secretly Talk to and Share with Each Other." The Kid Should See This. https://thekidshouldseethis.com/post/the-wood-wide-web -how-trees-secretly-talk-to-and-share-with-each-other.

BLOGS AND WEBSITES

Cornell Mushroom Blog
Edited by Dr. Kathie T. Hodge, associate professor of mycology at Cornell University
https://blog.mycology.cornell.edu

Ecovative
Sustainable mycelium-based products and alternative to plastics
https://www.ecovative.com

Fungi Perfecti
Features articles written by Paul Stamets, a well-known mycologist
https://fungi.com/blogs/articles/tagged/articles -by-paul-stamets

LIVIN Studio
Projects include the Fungi Mutarium, a prototype for converting plastic to edible fungi
https://www.livinstudio.com/fungi-mutarium

MushroomExpert.Com
Developed by Michael Kuo, an English teacher and amateur mycologist
https://www.mushroomexpert.com

Mushroom Observer
A website to record observations about mushrooms
https://mushroomobserver.org

Mycoworks
Mycelium-based leather alternative
https://www.mycoworks.com